EMMANUEL JOSEPH

Examining Your Company to Fuel Success

Contents

1

Chapter 1: Understanding the Market Landscape

The business world is akin to an ever-changing landscape, shaped by market trends, consumer behavior, and competitive dynamics. A comprehensive understanding of these elements is paramount for any business aspiring to thrive. Market trends provide insight into the shifting demands and preferences of consumers, while competitive dynamics reveal the strengths and weaknesses of industry players. By thoroughly analyzing these factors, businesses can identify potential opportunities and threats, enabling them to strategize effectively.

In addition, understanding the market landscape involves recognizing the impact of technological advancements on traditional business models. Innovations in technology can disrupt established practices, creating new avenues for growth or rendering existing strategies obsolete. Therefore, businesses must stay informed about emerging technologies and their potential implications. This knowledge allows them to adapt swiftly and leverage technological advancements to their advantage.

Moreover, the market landscape is influenced by macroeconomic factors such as economic growth, inflation rates, and government policies. These elements can significantly affect consumer purchasing power and business operations. By monitoring and analyzing these factors, businesses can anticipate changes in the economic environment and adjust their strategies accordingly. This proactive approach ensures that they remain resilient and competitive in a dynamic market.

2

Chapter 2: Identifying Core Competencies

Core competencies are the unique strengths and capabilities that distinguish a business from its competitors. Identifying these competencies is crucial for developing a competitive advantage. This process involves a thorough assessment of internal resources, skills, and expertise. By recognizing their core competencies, businesses can focus on what they do best, creating a value proposition that is difficult for others to replicate.

Once core competencies are identified, businesses can align their strategies to capitalize on these strengths. For instance, a company with exceptional customer service can build its brand around providing an unparalleled customer experience. Similarly, a business with advanced technological capabilities can innovate and develop cutting-edge products. By leveraging their core competencies, businesses can differentiate themselves in the market and achieve sustainable growth.

Furthermore, core competencies should be continually developed and nurtured. The business environment is constantly evolving, and staying ahead requires ongoing investment in key areas of strength. This may involve training and development programs, research and development initiatives, or strategic partnerships. By continually enhancing their core competencies, businesses can maintain their competitive edge and drive long-term success.

3

Chapter 3: Setting Clear Goals and Objectives

Setting clear and achievable goals is the cornerstone of any successful growth strategy. Goals provide direction and motivation for the entire organization, ensuring that everyone is working towards a common purpose. Well-defined objectives also serve as benchmarks for measuring progress and success, enabling businesses to track their performance and make necessary adjustments.

To set effective goals, businesses should adopt the SMART (Specific, Measurable, Achievable, Relevant, and Time-bound) framework. This approach ensures that goals are clearly defined and attainable within a specified timeframe. For example, instead of setting a vague goal like "increase sales," a SMART goal would be "increase sales by 20% within the next six months through targeted marketing campaigns." This specificity provides a clear roadmap for achieving the desired outcome.

In addition to setting short-term goals, businesses should also establish long-term objectives that align with their vision and mission. These overarching goals provide a sense of purpose and direction, guiding strategic decisions and actions. By balancing short-term and long-term objectives, businesses can drive immediate results while building a foundation for sustained growth.

Chapter 4: Crafting a Strategic Plan

A strategic plan is the blueprint for achieving business growth. It involves a detailed analysis of the current business environment, including a SWOT (Strengths, Weaknesses, Opportunities, and Threats) analysis. This assessment helps businesses identify their internal capabilities and external opportunities, as well as potential challenges they may face. By understanding these factors, businesses can develop a strategic plan that capitalizes on their strengths and addresses their weaknesses.

The strategic plan should outline specific initiatives and actions that the business will undertake to achieve its growth objectives. These initiatives should be aligned with the company's goals and core competencies, ensuring that resources are allocated effectively. For instance, a business may decide to invest in new technology, expand into new markets, or enhance its product offerings. By prioritizing and implementing these initiatives, businesses can drive growth and achieve their desired outcomes.

Moreover, the strategic plan should include a timeline for implementation and regular review intervals. This ensures that progress is monitored and adjustments are made as needed. The business environment is dynamic, and a flexible strategic plan allows businesses to adapt to changing conditions and seize new opportunities. By following a structured approach to strategic planning, businesses can navigate the complexities of growth and achieve long-term success.

5

Chapter 5: Leveraging Technology for Growth

In today's digital age, technology plays a pivotal role in business growth. It offers numerous opportunities for innovation, efficiency, and competitive advantage. By leveraging technology, businesses can streamline their operations, enhance productivity, and deliver better products and services. For example, automation can reduce manual processes, freeing up time and resources for more strategic activities. Similarly, data analytics can provide valuable insights into customer behavior, enabling businesses to make informed decisions and personalize their offerings.

In addition, technology can help businesses reach a wider audience and build stronger customer relationships. Digital marketing strategies, such as social media marketing, search engine optimization, and email campaigns, can effectively promote products and services to a global audience. By engaging with customers online, businesses can build brand awareness, foster loyalty, and drive sales. Furthermore, technology enables businesses to offer a seamless and convenient customer experience, from online shopping to personalized recommendations.

Moreover, staying abreast of technological advancements is essential for maintaining a competitive edge. Emerging technologies, such as artificial intelligence, blockchain, and the Internet of Things, have the potential to disrupt industries and create new opportunities. By continuously exploring and adopting these technologies, businesses can stay ahead of the curve and drive innovation. Investing in technology not only enhances current operations but also positions businesses for future growth and success.

6

Chapter 6: Building a Strong Brand Identity

A strong brand identity is a powerful asset that can drive business growth and success. It involves creating a distinct and memorable brand that resonates with customers and sets the business apart from its competitors. A compelling brand identity encompasses a clear and consistent message, a unique visual identity, and a strong value proposition. By investing in branding efforts, businesses can build trust and loyalty among their target audience.

To build a strong brand identity, businesses must first define their brand values and mission. These foundational elements guide all branding efforts and ensure consistency across all touchpoints. For example, a business that values sustainability should reflect this commitment in its messaging, product offerings, and operations. By staying true to its values, the business can build a genuine and authentic brand that customers relate to and support.

In addition, effective branding involves creating a distinct visual identity, including a logo, color scheme, and design elements. These visual components should be consistent across all marketing materials and communications, creating a cohesive and recognizable brand image. By maintaining a strong visual identity, businesses can enhance brand recognition and recall, making it easier for customers to identify and connect with the brand.

7

Chapter 7: Enhancing Customer Experience

Customer experience is a critical factor in driving business growth. It encompasses every interaction a customer has with a business, from the initial contact to post-purchase support. Delivering exceptional customer experiences is essential for building customer loyalty, encouraging repeat business, and generating positive word-of-mouth. By understanding and exceeding customer expectations, businesses can differentiate themselves and create lasting relationships.

To enhance customer experience, businesses must first understand customer needs and preferences. This involves gathering and analyzing customer feedback, conducting surveys, and monitoring online reviews. By gaining insights into what customers value, businesses can tailor their products, services, and interactions to meet and exceed expectations. Additionally, personalizing the customer experience, such as offering customized recommendations or personalized communication, can further enhance satisfaction and loyalty.

Moreover, optimizing every touchpoint in the customer journey is essential for delivering a seamless and positive experience. This includes ensuring a user-friendly website, providing prompt and helpful customer support, and maintaining high-quality products and services. By prioritizing customer satisfaction at every stage, businesses can create a positive and memorable experience that encourages repeat business and fosters long-term loyalty.

8

Chapter 8: Expanding Market Reach

E xpanding market reach is a key driver of business growth. It involves reaching new customer segments, entering new geographical markets, or diversifying product or service offerings. By strategically expanding market reach, businesses can increase their customer base, boost sales, and enhance their competitive position. This chapter explores various strategies for market expansion and provides insights into how businesses can successfully navigate this process.

One effective strategy for expanding market reach is geographical expansion. This involves entering new regions or countries where there is demand for the business's products or services. Geographical expansion requires thorough market research to understand the target market's needs, preferences, and regulatory environment. By tailoring their offerings and marketing strategies to the local market, businesses can effectively penetrate new regions and drive growth.

Another strategy is targeting new customer segments. This involves identifying and reaching customer groups that were previously untapped or underserved. For example, a business that primarily serves young adults may expand its offerings to cater to families or older adults. By diversifying their customer base, businesses can reduce dependence on a single market segment and increase their overall market share.

9

Chapter 9: Optimizing Operational Efficiency

Operational efficiency is essential for sustaining business growth. It involves streamlining processes, eliminating inefficiencies, and optimizing resources to enhance productivity and reduce costs. By focusing on operational efficiency, businesses can improve their bottom line, enhance customer satisfaction, and create a strong foundation for growth. This chapter explores strategies for achieving operational efficiency and provides insights into how businesses can continuously improve their operations.

One approach to optimizing operational efficiency is process automation. By automating repetitive and time-consuming tasks, businesses can free up time and resources for more strategic activities. Automation can also reduce the risk of errors, enhance accuracy, and improve overall efficiency. For example, automating inventory management, order processing, and customer support can streamline operations and improve service levels.

In addition to process automation, businesses can implement lean management practices to optimize efficiency. Lean management focuses on eliminating waste and improving processes to create value for customers. This approach involves identifying and addressing inefficiencies, such as unnecessary steps, delays, and defects. By continuously improving processes and reducing waste, businesses can enhance their overall efficiency and productivity.

Another strategy for optimizing operational efficiency is continuous improvement. This involves regularly evaluating and refining processes to ensure they remain effective and efficient. Businesses can implement methodologies such as Six Sigma or Total Quality Management to drive continuous improvement. By fostering a culture of continuous improvement, businesses can adapt to changing conditions, address emerging challenges, and maintain a high level of operational efficiency.

10

Chapter 10: Fostering Innovation and Creativity

Innovation and creativity are essential for driving business growth and staying competitive. This chapter explores the ways in which businesses can foster a culture of innovation and encourage creative thinking. By embracing a mindset of continuous improvement and experimentation, businesses can develop new ideas and solutions that drive growth. Additionally, creating an environment that supports collaboration and encourages risk-taking can lead to breakthrough innovations.

To foster innovation, businesses should create a supportive and inclusive environment where employees feel empowered to share their ideas. This involves encouraging open communication, providing opportunities for brainstorming and collaboration, and recognizing and rewarding innovative contributions. By valuing and promoting creativity, businesses can tap into the diverse perspectives and talents of their workforce.

Moreover, businesses can invest in research and development (R&D) to drive innovation. R&D initiatives enable businesses to explore new technologies, develop new products and services, and improve existing offerings. By allocating resources to R&D, businesses can stay at the forefront of industry advancements and seize new opportunities for growth. Additionally, partnerships with external organizations, such as universities or research institutions, can provide access to new knowledge and expertise, further driving innovation.

11

Chapter 11: Measuring and Evaluating Performance

easuring and evaluating performance is crucial for understanding the effectiveness of growth strategies. This chapter outlines the key metrics and performance indicators that businesses should track to gauge their progress. By regularly monitoring performance, businesses can identify areas of improvement and make data-driven decisions. Additionally, performance evaluation provides insights into the impact of growth initiatives and helps businesses stay on track to achieve their goals.

Key performance indicators (KPIs) are essential tools for measuring business performance. These metrics can include financial indicators, such as revenue growth, profit margins, and return on investment, as well as non-financial indicators, such as customer satisfaction, employee engagement, and operational efficiency. By tracking KPIs, businesses can gain a comprehensive view of their performance and identify areas that require attention.

Regular performance reviews and evaluations are also important for continuous improvement. These reviews involve analyzing performance data, identifying trends and patterns, and assessing the effectiveness of growth strategies. By conducting regular performance evaluations, businesses can make informed decisions, adjust their strategies as needed, and ensure that they are on the path to achieving their growth objectives.

12

Chapter 12: Adapting to Change and Future Planning

I n the dynamic business environment, the ability to adapt to change is essential for sustained growth. This chapter focuses on the importance of agility and future planning in business success. By staying attuned to market trends and being responsive to changes, businesses can navigate uncertainties and seize new opportunities. Future planning involves anticipating potential challenges and developing strategies to mitigate risks. By fostering a culture of adaptability and forward-thinking, businesses can ensure their continued growth and success in an ever-changing landscape.

To effectively adapt to change, businesses must develop a flexible and resilient organizational structure. This involves building a culture that embraces change and encourages continuous learning and development. By promoting agility and innovation, businesses can quickly respond to market shifts and capitalize on emerging opportunities. Additionally, businesses should establish contingency plans to address potential disruptions and ensure business continuity.

Future planning also involves setting long-term goals and developing strategies to achieve them. This includes identifying potential growth opportunities, exploring new markets, and investing in new technologies. By taking a proactive approach to future planning, businesses can position themselves for long-term success and maintain their competitive edge. By continuously evaluating and adjusting their strategies, businesses can adapt to the evolving business landscape and achieve sustained growth.